NORTH DAKOTA

Past and Present

Mark J. Lewis

New York

Dedicated to learning for learning's sake

Published in 2011 by The Rosen Publishing Group, Inc.
29 East 21st Street, New York, NY 10010

First Edition

Library of Congress Cataloging-in-Publication Data

Lewis, Mark J.
North Dakota: past and present / Mark J. Lewis. — 1st ed.
    p. cm. — (The United States—past and present)
Includes bibliographical references and index.
ISBN 978-1-4358-9492-1 (library binding)
ISBN 978-1-4358-9519-5 (pbk.)
ISBN 978-1-4358-9553-9 (6-pack)
1. North Dakota—Juvenile literature. I. Title.
F636.3.L49 2010
978.4—dc22

                                                                2010002697

Manufactured in Malaysia

CPSIA Compliance Information: Batch #S10YA: For further information, contact Rosen Publishing, New York, New York, at 1-800-237-9932.

On the cover: Top left: Fort Union Trading Post National Historic Site includes within its walls the Fort Union Trading Post, which was vital for trading on the upper Missouri River in the 1800s. Top right: This harvester is filling a tractor-trailer with a field crop on a North Dakota farm. Bottom: This Badlands landscape is in Theodore Roosevelt National Park, North Dakota.

Contents

Introduction   5

Chapter 1
The Geography of North Dakota   6

Chapter 2
The History of North Dakota   12

Chapter 3
The Government of North Dakota   19

Chapter 4
The Economy of North Dakota   25

Chapter 5
**People from North Dakota:
Past and Present**   30

Timeline   38

North Dakota at a Glance   39

Glossary   41

For More Information   43

For Further Reading   45

Bibliography   46

Index   47

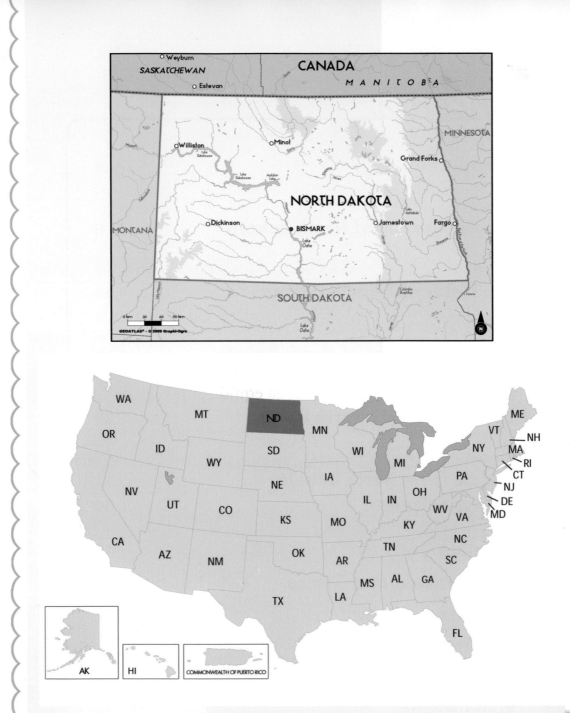

Top: North Dakota is shown with neighboring states and provinces and its state capital, Bismarck. Bottom: The nineteenth-largest state's location is highlighted on a U.S. map.

Introduction

On a U.S. map, the rectangle at the top center is North Dakota. North Dakota has the honor of being at the geographic center of the North American continent. The small city of Rugby has a monument claiming the location is equidistant from the Atlantic, Pacific, and Arctic oceans, as well as the Gulf of Mexico.

North Dakota borders Canada to the north, South Dakota to the south, Minnesota to the west, and Montana to the east. North Dakota is the nineteenth-largest state, measuring 340 miles (547 kilometers) long and 211 miles (240 km) wide. The steep buttes, rolling prairies, and low rich valleys cover an area of 70,704 square miles (11,3787 square km).

North Dakota is an agricultural state. Farming shapes North Dakota's economy, its politics, its culture, and its citizens. Many Native American tribes farmed there for hundreds of years. The rich black soil and fertile flatlands of the Red River Valley are the features for which the state is best known.

North Dakota has been home to Theodore Roosevelt, who lived in the Dakota Territory for a few years before becoming president of the United States. Phil Jackson, a great coach of the National Basketball Association (NBA), attended high school in North Dakota. The state has seen the rise of the Non-Partisan League, a powerful socialist organization unusual in the United States, and the fall of Native American leaders Sitting Bull and Crazy Horse.

Chapter 1

THE GEOGRAPHY OF NORTH DAKOTA

Seventeen hundred square miles (2,736 sq km) of North Dakota are covered by lakes and rivers. The Missouri River, which is the longest river in the United States, the Red River (sometimes called Red River of the North), Lake Sakakawea, and Lake Oahe are major water resources.

North Dakota is a relatively flat state. White Butte, however, rises to an altitude of 3,506 feet (1,069 meters) above sea level, the highest point in the state. The lowest point of the state lies along the Red River, at 750 feet (229 m) above sea level.

Regions of North Dakota

North Dakota has three geographic regions: the Missouri Plateau, the Drift Prairie, and the Red River Valley.

The Missouri Plateau

The Missouri Plateau takes up the western third of North Dakota. The Missouri River runs southeast across the plateau. The third-largest man-made lake in the United States, Lake Sakakawea was formed when the Missouri River was dammed in 1956. The lake is 180 miles (290 km) long. The northern portion of the plateau was worn down

Bison still roam parts of North Dakota, including the Theodore Roosevelt National Park in the Badlands. The region of the Badlands is dry and hilly and lies in the western part of the state.

to rolling hills and shallow lakes, called kettle lakes. The southern portion of the plateau, called the Badlands, is too dry for much plant growth. Without plants holding the dry soil, there has been a great deal of erosion. The landscape is a series of sharp ravines and colorful cliff faces carved away by wind and water.

The Missouri Plateau has a semiarid climate, meaning it is quite dry. North Dakota is one of the driest states in the country, and the plateau is the driest part of the state. There is very little farming done there.

The Missouri Plateau is rich in wildlife. Tourists can see bobcats, rattlesnakes, bison, and wild turkeys. Hunters can find ring-necked

Lake Agassiz

If explorers had mapped the North Dakota of ten thousand years ago, they would show a different state, with the eastern region largely under water. Between thirty thousand and ten thousand years ago, much of the state was covered by huge sheets of ice—the Dakota and Minnesota glaciers. As the Ice Age came to a close, the glaciers melted. Water drained into the lowlands that now form the Red River Valley. Waters also covered much of western Minnesota, eastern North Dakota, southwestern Ontario, and southern Manitoba, though not all at the same time.

William Keating, an American geologist, first suggested the existence of this body of water in 1823. It was Swiss geologist and naturalist Louis Agassiz (1807–1873), however, who linked the lake's existence and demise to glacial action. The lake was named in his honor in 1879. At its largest, Lake Agassiz would have been larger than all the Great Lakes combined and would have contained more fresh water than all the lakes now on the planet! Beaches of the once giant lake still remain, miles from any existing lake. The mammoth lake drained through either the Mississippi River by way of the Minnesota River or the Great Lakes and into the Hudson Bay and the Atlantic Ocean. Today, hundreds—if not thousands—of lakes and ponds remain in the region, the deepest relics of Lake Agassiz. Some of these bodies of water include Lake Winnipeg, Winnipegosis, and Manitoba, and Lake of the Woods. The nutrients that once dissolved in the water now mix with silt from the former lakebed to form the Red River Valley's farmlands. The rich black soils that the ancient lake deposited have made the region one of the best wheat-growing areas in North America.

pheasants. Lake Sakakawea is rich with salmon and walleye, which make the area a popular location for sport fishing. The lake attracts a number of endangered bird species such as the piping plover and the extremely rare golden eagle, the world's largest raptor.

The land is mostly grassland, natural habitat for the grazers that live there. There are more than four hundred species of plants in this region. Juniper trees provide shade in the summer, and their berries are a critical source of food for birds in the winter.

The golden eagle hunts fish and wildlife along North Dakota's Missouri Plateau.

The Drift Prairie

The Drift Prairie region takes up central North Dakota. Rolling hills have been flattened by massive glaciers from the last ice age. The name "drift" comes from the fact that the soil is mostly glacial drift, which is a mix of sand, gravel, and clay. This soil is good for growing not only prairie grass, but also wheat and other grains that make up much of the state's farming industry.

In the northern part of the region rise the Turtle Mountains. Most of the state's few forests are in the Turtle Mountain area.

Central North Dakota gets more precipitation than the western part of the state. Most is in the form of snow. Bismarck, the capital of

North Dakota, is in the Drift Prairie region. The city averages 42 inches (107 centimeters) of snowfall annually. Winter temperatures plunge to as low as -66 degrees Fahrenheit (-54 degrees Celsius). By July and August, temperatures may reach a blazing 121°F (49°C). The amazingly wide variation in temperature is the third widest in the nation. This occurs because of North Dakota's distance from an ocean or large lake. Large bodies of water moderate the climate.

The prairie grass growing in the Drift region is perfect for grazing cattle. Huge herds of bison once roamed the area. Though hunted nearly to extinction, they are now protected by law. Other animals that live in the region are the endangered whooping crane and the world's fastest flying bird, the peregrine falcon, which dives down on prey at more than 180 miles (290 kilometers) per hour.

There are also beautiful wildflowers and cacti that live on the prairie. The wild prairie rose, North Dakota's state flower, is an important source of nectar for prairie bees. The prairie crocus, a small purple-white flower, sprouts in tight groups.

The Red River Valley

The easternmost region of North Dakota is the Red River Valley. The flat fields and rolling hills, worn smooth by glaciers, are the most populous part of the state. Fargo and Grand Forks, two of the largest cities in the state, lie along the Red River. This area is the lowest part of North Dakota. The basin, once grassland, is now mostly farmland. The basin is the remainder of a glacial lake, which is a lake formed by the melted waters from the last ice age. The mineral-rich silt that fell to the bottom of that lake left behind fertile soil. The basin is drained by the Red River, which runs along the North Dakota-Minnesota border. Devils Lake is another important source of water for this agricultural region. It is the largest natural lake in North Dakota.

Wheat is one of the largest crops grown in North Dakota's Red River Valley. Large combines make huge harvests fast and economical.

The Red River Valley receives more rain than the other two regions of the state. Drought, however, may still cause crop loss during some years.

The wetlands along the Red River form an important habitat for many species in North Dakota. The beautiful wood duck (popular with hunters), herds of elk, and the colorful tiger salamander make their homes here. These wetlands, however, are rapidly being lost to farmland conversion, pollution, and illegal dumping. It is important to strike a balance between the needs of humans and the needs of the environment in the near future.

Chapter 2

THE HISTORY OF NORTH DAKOTA

The first people to live in the area that is now North Dakota were hunters. They hunted the woolly mammoth and the giant bison using tools made from flint and obsidian. Scientific evidence suggests that these people died off suddenly for mysterious reasons.

Native Americans

In the fifteenth century, Native Americans moved into the area. The Mandan were an agrarian society. They lived in earthen lodges in farming villages along the Missouri, Knife, and Heart rivers. A very social people, the Mandan formed important relationships with European settlers. The Lakota-Sioux came to the Dakota Territory in the early eighteenth century. They also traded with European settlers, who gave them horses. The Cheyenne came to the area when the migrating Lakota and Ojibwa forced them westward. They replaced their earthen lodges with teepees and took on a plains lifestyle, following the herds of bison and eating wild fruits and vegetables. They traded with the Spanish. The Assiniboin were another seminomadic plains people. They followed herds of bison in summer and traded heavily with Europeans, both directly and through the Mandan. They roamed western North Dakota along the Knife River, fishing as well as hunting.

European Settlement

In 1610, Henry Hudson claimed the Hudson Bay watershed for England. This area included a large part of eastern North Dakota. Explorer René-Robert Cavelier, Sieur de La Salle claimed the Missouri River area for France in 1682. In 1738, French Canadian explorer Pierre Gaultier de Varennes, Sieur de La Vérendrye traveled to Mandan villages and started important trading.

By 1781, fur trappers from England and France had moved to the area. With the help of the Mandan, they began trapping and trading pelts of beavers, otters, mink, and foxes. In 1794, French

The Mandan helped European settlers by acting as guides and translators. Sadly, though, they eventually had their land taken from them by settlers.

trader René Jusseaume established the first European fur trading post by the Knife River. Fur traders founded the first white settlement in North Dakota, in Pembina, in 1801.

With the purchase of the Louisiana Territory by the United States in 1803, Meriwether Lewis and William Clark went to look for the Northwest Passage. They spent the winter with the Mandan along the Missouri River. This is where the travelers met Sacagawea. She would act as a guide and translator during the next two years of their journey.

Native Americans in North Dakota

In the early history of the United States, the Sioux had helped the British in the Revolutionary War (1775–1783) but eventually signed peace treaties with the United States. The ever-increasing flow of settlers into North Dakota created tension with Native Americans. Settlers moved onto Sioux land and claimed it outright as their own. The U.S. Army built forts to protect settlers and traders. There were several major battles with the Sioux. In 1863, the army pushed the Sioux across the Missouri River. Some of the Sioux signed treaties and, in 1867, the Fort Totten Indian Reservation was established. Many tribes, however, simply refused to sign treaties or they abandoned reservations.

In 1867, the U.S. government and the Sioux signed a treaty giving the Sioux possession of the area known as the Black Hills, in what is now South Dakota. The United States immediately violated the treaty, however, when prospectors discovered gold in the area.

In the resulting fight, Sitting Bull, a Sioux medicine man, and Crazy Horse, a Sioux chief, led a force against General George Custer at Little Bighorn. They beat the U.S. Army decisively in 1876. Though the fighting would continue for decades, the U.S. Army, which had finished fighting the Civil War (1861–1865), poured troops and resources into the area. By 1890, Sitting Bull had been killed and the last of the Sioux either agreed to live on reservations or were killed.

Today, approximately twenty thousand Native Americans live on reservations in North Dakota. More than eight thousand Chippewas and other Native Americans live on the Turtle Mountain Indian Reservation. In 1996, the Chippewas erected the first wind turbine on a reservation. They use this turbine to power some businesses, including a casino. The Three Affiliated Tribes is a union of Mandan, Hidatsa, and Arikara peoples living along the Missouri River. They live by selling oil, natural gas, and mining rights to private businesses and the federal government.

In 1818, North Dakota became part of what would be known as the Missouri Territory. The American Fur Company, one of the largest businesses in the United States at that time, opened Fort Union Trading Post along the Missouri River in 1828. When gold was discovered in California in 1848, Congress organized a number of other territories to keep the gold under the control of the United States.

A Norwegian family is photographed near their sod house in Milton, North Dakota. The Homestead Act made it possible for immigrants with little money to settle in North Dakota.

This organization of the lands drew still more settlers west. On March 2, 1861, President James Buchanan established the Dakota Territory. This area included parts of what are today North Dakota, South Dakota, Wyoming, and Montana.

The Homestead Act

In 1862, President Abraham Lincoln signed into law the Homestead Act. This law granted 160 acres (65 hectares) of land to anyone who would live on the land for five years. The act enabled farmers to move west and settle in the Dakota Territory.

Meanwhile, many immigrants were coming to live in the United States from Germany and Norway. Jobs in these countries were scarce, leaving many people out of work. Minorities in Norway and Germany were also suffering from religious oppression. In the

The railroads, such as the Northern Pacific, made it possible for farmers to move crops to cities for sale. They also allowed railroad owners to control crop prices, hurting farmers' profits.

next decade, a million Germans and thousands of Norwegians immigrated to the United States, seeking a better life. They were drawn to North Dakota by the nearly endless supply of cheap productive farmland. Today, almost one-third of all North Dakota residents are of Norwegian descent, which is more than any other state!

Statehood

On February 22, 1889, Congress passed the Enabling Act, granting statehood to North Dakota, South Dakota, Montana, and Washington. On November 2, 1889, President Benjamin Harrison signed an act proclaiming North Dakota as the thirty-ninth state.

With statehood, the Republican Party gained power. Republican John Miller was elected governor. Owners of the Canadian Pacific Railway, the Northern Pacific Railway, and the Great Northern Railway held major influence with the Republican Party. These companies owned the means of transportation for farm products. They also owned the grain elevators, where wheat was stored. Farmers worried that the Republicans would gain control of the price of grain, costing the farmers a lot of money.

Farmers united to create the Farmers Alliance. This organization was like a union. It gave the farmers power to refuse to sell their grain if they did not like the price that was offered. The struggle over grain prices continues today, except that it has lessened. State and federal governments monitor trade and vigorously guard against price fixing and monopolies.

The Non-Partisan League

The fears that led to the formation of the Farmers Alliance also led to the creation of a political party called the Non-Partisan League (NPL). Farmers were frustrated that the railroads and banks had so much power. They joined the NPL and elected candidates to state office in the 1918 elections. The state government then authorized the control of grain elevators by the state. With the support of the NPL the state legislature also created a state bank.

The NPL lost power when grain prices fell in the 1920s. Private banks rejected the state-owned bank. An investigation found that it had run out of money. The NPL governor was removed from office. North Dakota voters did elect another NPL governor, who later became a U.S. senator in Washington, D.C. The NPL, however, lost power and merged with the Democratic Party in 1956.

Fargo

In 1871, a small city was founded when some immigrants settled on land where the Northern Pacific Railway crossed the Red River. This city was named Fargo, after the director of the Northern Pacific Railway, William G. Fargo. Surrounded by flat, fertile fields, the small town grew rapidly.

Fargo, despite often extreme weather, is a bustling economic center and is North Dakota's largest city, with more than ninety-nine thousand people.

In 1893, a fire spread until it destroyed nearly all of Fargo's downtown. Amazingly, the citizens rebuilt nearly all of the damaged area within a year. A powerful tornado destroyed much of the northern part of the city in 1957. Still, the city prospered. The North Dakota State Agricultural College, now known as North Dakota State University, is located in Fargo. The giant computer corporation Microsoft has a regional office downtown. Fargo is North Dakota's largest city and has been listed as one of the nation's most livable cities. It is a symbol of what the state has grown to be: a successful and economically diverse powerhouse.

Chapter 3

THE GOVERNMENT OF NORTH DAKOTA

The government of North Dakota is built around the state constitution, which was adopted in 1889. This document, which has power over all state law, lays out a set of principles that all state law must follow. North Dakota's constitution also creates the state government by the people. That government has three branches: the executive, the legislative, and the judicial.

Executive Branch

The head of the executive branch of the government is the governor. The governor is elected by the citizens of North Dakota for a four-year term. The governor may run for election and reelection for as many terms as he or she wishes. The state governor has the power to sign legislative bills to make them law. He or she can also veto bills, stopping them from becoming law. The governor may introduce new legislation. He or she is also chair of the North Dakota Industrial Commission, which regulates the drilling for oil and natural gas within the state. The governor has the important ability to influence the voters and legislators because people pay attention to what the governor says about certain issues. The governor lives in Bismarck, next to the State Capitol Building, in the

The State Capitol Building, the skyscraper seen here, in Bismarck, houses the office of the governor, the office of the lieutenant governor, and both houses of the legislature.

governor's official residence. He or she has an office in the State Capitol Building.

Another position in the executive branch is the lieutenant governor. This official has the job of acting as president of the senate, giving the lieutenant governor some power over lawmaking. For much of the state's history, the lieutenant governor was elected separately from the governor. This circumstance meant that the two officials might be of opposing political parties, which created a great deal of friction within the executive branch. That was changed in 1974 so that the governor and lieutenant governor were elected together, much like the president and vice president in a national election.

Other elected positions within the executive branch are the secretary of state and attorney general. There are also state commissioners, who are appointed by the governor. The commissioners are in charge of state agriculture, labor, insurance, taxes, and public service.

Legislature

The state legislature is called the legislative assembly. The legislative assembly is a bicameral system, meaning it has two parts: the house of representatives and the senate. There are forty-seven districts within the state. Each district is represented by two representatives and one senator. The representa-

The governor may address the legislature to help the lawmaking branch of government understand his or her executive programs.

tives each serve a two-year term. The senators are elected to a four-year term.

Members of both houses may introduce, speak about, and vote on legislation. A major part of that legislation is the state budget. Members help write the legislation that decides how much of the state's tax revenue goes to various programs and causes, like school building, road maintenance, and social programs such as welfare. The houses meet in the State Capitol Building in Bismarck for eighty days in odd-numbered years. For example, the assembly for 2011 will

PAST AND PRESENT

The State-Owned Bank

One important and unusual part of North Dakota's government is the state-owned bank, which is the only such bank in the nation. The bank was created ninety years ago by the Non-Partisan League to make reasonably priced loans to farmers.

Farmers always needed to borrow money to purchase seed, machinery, and fertilizer. Before the Bank of North Dakota was formed, farmers relied on private banks. Some of those banks banded together, refusing to lend farmers money unless they paid extremely high interest payments. This practice is called predatory lending, and it drove many farmers out of business. The state-owned bank was formed to give low-interest loans when the private banks would not, preventing many farmers from going bankrupt. Farmers were then able to pay the money back after they sold the next year's crop. Overall, the Bank of North Dakota gave farmers some control over loans that were a very necessary part of the farming industry.

There are two groups of people in charge of running the Bank of North Dakota. The state industrial commission is made up of the governor, the attorney general, and the commissioner of agriculture. They are in charge of making general policy decisions, such as what interest rates to charge customers. The governor also names seven people to the advisory board. They evaluate the way the bank is lending money and make recommendations to the industrial commission on how to make the Bank of North Dakota more effective.

Although the practice of predatory lending is controlled today by state and federal laws, the Bank of North Dakota has taken on other roles in state finance. It lends money to students to help them pay for college. The bank also loans money to small businesses and to other banks. The money the bank collects on the interest from these loans raises money for the state treasury. In years of record bank losses and bank failures around the country, the Bank of North Dakota has posted record gains. By law, half of the bank's profit goes directly to the state. This money pays for public schools and state road-building projects. As a result, the state needs to charge its citizens fewer taxes in the next year.

meet beginning in January. They will finish their business in April. The legislative council takes care of daily business when the assembly is not in session. The legislative council is composed of seventeen legislators. Among them are the leaders of both parties for the house of representatives and the senate and the speaker of the house. The speaker of the house also appoints three representatives from each party to serve on the council. The lieutenant governor also appoints four senators from the majority party and two senators from the minority party to serve on the council.

North Dakota is represented in the federal government in Washington, D.C., by one representative and two senators. The state also casts three electoral votes in the electoral college.

Judicial Branch

The judicial branch of North Dakota's state government is charged with hearing criminal cases, civil cases, and any appeals to those case decisions. Criminal and civil cases are heard in municipal and district courts. Municipal courts hear cases involving violations of municipal ordinances, such as traffic violations or building codes. Judges are elected to a four-year term. District courts hear cases involving misdemeanors like theft and felony cases, such as assault or armed robbery. They also hear cases in juvenile courts. There are forty-two district judges spread across seven districts, the more populous districts having more judges. They are each elected for a six-year term. There are no term limits.

Any appeals to decisions by these courts go to the North Dakota Court of Appeals. This court is made up of groups of a three-member panel of district court judges, the state's supreme court justices, and attorneys. The case is ruled on or rejected. Any ruling made by the court of appeals may then be appealed to the state's supreme court.

The North Dakota Supreme Court is the highest court in the state. It is made up of five justices, who are elected for ten-year terms. The court does not hear cases with a jury and give a decision based on evidence. Instead, the job of the court is to decide on questions of law related to specific cases on appeal.

Local Government

North Dakota has fifty-three counties that manage issues such as local road construction, sewage, trash management, property rights, and some schools. Taxes pay for all of these things. These counties are run by a board of seven commissioners, who are elected for a four-year term.

Counties are divided into cities and townships. Cities, also known as municipalities, within those counties usually formed to keep control of their local area. In North Dakota, there are 360 municipalities with populations that range from Fargo's 99,000 people to Lehr's 114. A mayor with a city council runs each municipality.

Chapter 4

THE ECONOMY OF NORTH DAKOTA

The availability of land in North Dakota led to a phenomenon: the bonanza farm. Wealthy investors living on the East Coast would buy thousands of acres of land and then farm them using factory techniques. Large teams of horses would be hooked up to wide plows, called gang plows, and move straight across a field for 1 mile (1.6 km) or more tilling. The farm would employ hundreds of workers in the field and a staff similar to that of any factory, with mechanics, cooks, bookkeepers, and managers. Some of these farms had more than 64,000 acres (25,900 ha).

These bonanza farms were the minority of farms. Most of North Dakota's agricultural economy consisted of family-owned farms. Bonanza farms were proof that farming in North Dakota could be made to fit the factory style of work. Many of the money-saving practices in place on farms today took shape during the bonanza farm era.

Diversification

Moving into the later part of the twentieth century, North Dakota's economy began to diversify. This means the economy began to create businesses besides wheat farming. Although North Dakota

A bonanza farm near Hillsboro prepares its gang plow of more than seventy horses. The farm seen here, photographed in 1890, was one of the first in North Dakota to raise corn.

continued to produce massive wheat crops, farmers also planted soybeans and corn. Where wheat once made up nearly all of the money earned in North Dakota, today it only comprises one-quarter of farming profits. Farmers also found that they could leave their fields fallow for a few seasons while the cattle grazed the grass growing there. The cow manure fertilized the soil. Raising cattle is the second-most profitable farming commodity after wheat.

Other major farm products are soybeans, sugar beets, sunflowers, canola seeds, barley, and potatoes. This wide variety of produce keeps North Dakota safe from crop failure. If one crop has a bad year, there will be many other products for farmers to sell.

Manufacturing

Agriculture has always been the largest part of North Dakota's economy. It is an industry that requires plenty of equipment and raw materials. Much of that was, and still is, manufactured in North

Dakota. The cities of Fargo, Grand Forks, and Bismarck are the centers of manufacturing.

The largest share of manufacturing is food processing. Milk is pasteurized and packaged. Bread and pasta are made and shipped to all fifty states and nations around the world.

The second-largest portion of manufacturing is machinery. Farm equipment, such as tractors, combines, and plows, is made and assembled. It may be used in North Dakota or sold internationally. North Dakota also makes a large amount of construction machinery, such as cranes and bulldozers.

Though highly polluting, the coal mined in North Dakota provides jobs and energy for people around the state and across the country.

Mining

In the 1880s, North Dakota began mining lignite coal. This is a low-quality, highly polluting coal. It is easy to find in western North Dakota. The state now produces about 30,864,717 tons (28 million metric tonnes) per year, second only to Texas.

In 1951, oil was discovered in western North Dakota. Within three years, pumps and refineries were producing gasoline from that oil and more oil was being discovered. North Dakota currently produces 2 percent of the nation's petroleum.

The Family Farm

In the early days of the Dakota Territory, people came to farm the land. The size of an individual farm at the time varied depending on how many people were available to work the land. With the end of the Civil War and the passing of the Homestead Act, settlers were offered 65 acres (26 ha) of land. One family owned each portion.

The era of the bonanza farm showed that farming was not just a family business. These farms were often 50,000 acres (20,234 ha). In the early 1900s, land became too expensive for bonanza farming. These enormous farms were broken up and sold to family farmers. The average family farm grew to be about 400 acres (162 ha), but it was still owned and managed by the family.

During World War II (1939–1945), demand for wheat increased. Many farmers, however, were fighting in Europe or the Pacific. Women took on all the roles of running the farm. With the end of the war, men usually took back those responsibilities. But the war helped convince people that a woman could run a farm, or any business, just as well as a man could.

After the war, many people left farming. The farms were sold to the remaining farmers, making their farms larger. The size of the farm continued to grow until the 1990s, when it leveled off.

Although the majority of farms are owned by a family, they are not the family businesses of fifty years ago. Modern farming is much more industrial.

Farmers harvest wheat using a steam-powered thresher, which makes the operation quick and requires fewer employees.

North Dakota began producing natural gas from the oil wells. Companies also create synthetic natural gas from lignite coal. This is one way of getting clean energy from coal that continues to grow in popularity.

Service Sector

The other large sector of the economy in North Dakota is the service sector. Service workers do not manufacture products, such as oil or food. Instead, service workers accomplish a task like cutting hair, treating a sick patient, or programming a computer. Many service jobs involve fixing things, such as automobiles, farm equipment, or electronics.

For most of the state's history, the services that were provided helped farms succeed. This is no longer the case. The mining and manufacturing companies need service workers to keep their machines running and their computers programmed. There are also service companies that work for people in other states. Banks in North Dakota may lend money to other states or other nations over the Internet. Workers in the health care industry, an industry that includes many medical professionals, make up more than one-tenth of North Dakota's population!

Chapter 5

PEOPLE FROM NORTH DAKOTA:
PAST AND PRESENT

Numerous famous people have called North Dakota home at some point in their lives. The vast stretches of flat fields and the dramatic Badlands have affected future writers, singers, and even presidents.

Lynn Anderson (1947–) Lynn Anderson is a country music singer who has more than fifty Top 40 hit songs. In the 1970s, Anderson dominated the country music scene, winning a Grammy for her hit "I Never Promised You a Rose Garden." She was inducted into the American Country Music Association's Hall of Fame in 1999.

Anne Carlsen (1915–2002) Anne Carlsen was an educator and advocate for people with disabilities. Born without forearms or lower legs, Carlsen was encouraged by her family to play games with other children. In 1938, she accepted a job as a teacher at the School for Crippled Children in North Dakota. She eventually became principal, and later the superintendent. In 1958, she met Vice President Richard Nixon when she received the prestigious Handicapped American of the Year Award.

Lynn Anderson, shown here being honored in Nashville, Tennessee, is a widely known country singer from Grand Forks, North Dakota.

Ronald Davies (1904–1996) Ronald Davies was named U.S. District Court Judge for North Dakota by President Dwight Eisenhower in 1955. In 1957, he served temporarily in Arkansas, where he heard the case of *Aaron vs. Cooper*. His ruling prevented the governor of Arkansas from using the National Guard to stop nine black students from attending an all-white school. It was a major step in ending segregation. Davies was awarded the Martin Luther King Jr. Holiday Award and North Dakota's highest honor, the Theodore Roosevelt Rough Rider Award.

Sixty-eight years after his death, Carl "Ben" Eielson was given the Theodore Roosevelt Rough Rider Award for his 1928 flight over the North Pole.

Carl "Ben" Eielson (1897–1929) Ben Eielson, born in Hatton, became a pilot in the U.S. Army Air Service at the age of twenty. In 1928, he and another pilot flew 2,200 miles (3,541 km) from Alaska to Norway. Their long flight over the Atlantic Ocean was considered dangerous in that era. In 1929, Eielson died when his plane crashed in Siberia while on a rescue mission to save people stranded on a ship in the Bering Strait.

Famous Leaders in North Dakota

These three leaders are just a few of the many who have contributed to North Dakota's past and present.

Warren Christopher (1925–) Born in Scranton, Warren Christopher has served as a deputy attorney general, deputy secretary of state, and secretary of state. During his time leading the U.S. State Department (1993–1997), he helped engineer the Oslo Peace Accords, an important treaty between Israel and the Palestine Liberation Organization. He also helped improve U.S. relations with China. Today, Christopher teaches international affairs at the University of California, Los Angeles.

Theodore Roosevelt (1858–1919) Theodore Roosevelt triumphed over illness and became a champion of the outdoors. After his wife and mother both died, Roosevelt retreated to North Dakota, where he had already established two cattle ranches near Medora. He became president of the United States at age forty-two, with the assassination of William McKinley in 1901. Roosevelt was known for fighting corruption and trying to give power to the people. He was quoted as saying, "If it were not for my years in North Dakota, I would never have become president of the United States."

Sitting Bull (1831–1890) Sitting Bull, known as Tatanka Iyotaka by his people, was a chief with the Lakota-Sioux tribe. He is remembered for his spiritual wisdom and legendary courage. In 1876, Sitting Bull had a vision that several area tribes would be attacked by European Americans. His troops launched a surprise attack on their invaders and defeated them. He lived the last years of his life at Standing Rock Sioux Reservation, near Fort Yates. In 1996, Standing Rock College changed its name to Sitting Bull College to honor the heroic leader.

Phil Jackson (1945–) Phil Jackson grew up in Williston, North Dakota. He played basketball for Williston High School and for the University of North Dakota. As a professional, he played with the New York Knicks. Jackson became the most successful coach in the history of the NBA by leading the Chicago Bulls and the Los Angeles Lakers to numerous championships. His coaching style is credited with helping many great basketball players, including Michael Jordan, Shaquille O'Neal, and Kobe Bryant.

Louis L'Amour (1908–1988) Louis L'Amour, born in Jamestown, was the author of more than one hundred western fiction and cowboy stories. He traveled the world as a hobo, a soldier, and a laborer and his writings reflect the simple life he encountered. In 1984, President Ronald Reagan awarded L'Amour the Medal of Freedom for his lifetime achievements.

Kellan Lutz (1985–) Actor Kellan Lutz was born in Dickinson. He has appeared in small roles in several television shows, including *The Bold and the Beautiful*, *CSI*, and *Heroes*. He is most famous for his role as Emmett Cullen in the film adaptations of the Twilight book series by Stephenie Meyers.

Clifford "Fido" Purpur (1912–2001) Fido Purpur, born in Grand Forks, was the first North Dakotan to play in the National Hockey League (NHL). Purpur joined the St. Louis Eagles in 1934. He was nicknamed Fido because one sportswriter compared Purpur's skill for covering the rink quickly

Louis L' Amour was an eager reader as a child and frequently listened to wandering cowboys who told stories of life on the American frontier.

to that of a hunting dog in a field of pheasants. Purpur was inducted into the U.S. Hockey Hall of Fame in 1974.

James Rosenquist (1933–)
Born in Grand Forks, James Rosenquist began his pop art career by winning a scholarship to the acclaimed Minneapolis School of Art. After Rosenquist went to art school in college, he exploded onto the modern art scene with angular images that used common objects like detergent bottles and U-Haul trailers to tell stories and express emotion. In addition to painting, Rosenquist has created countless prints and drawings. He has been compared to pop art legend Andy Warhol. New York's Solomon R. Guggenheim Museum held an exhibition of Rosenquist's work in 2003. The exhibition also traveled to the Guggenheim Museum in Bilbao, Spain. In 2009, a brush fire destroyed Rosenquist's home, office, and art studio in Aripeka, Florida. One of the paintings that was destroyed in the fire was a mural for the Plains Art Museum

James Rosenquist began painting as a child in Grand Forks. He is shown here in front of one of his paintings.

in Fargo. Rosenquist repainted the mural, which includes North Dakota subjects such as the meadowlark and state seal, for the museum.

Sacagawea (c. 1790–1812) Sacagawea was a translator and guide on the Lewis and Clark expedition. She gave birth to a baby boy in 1803 shortly before the expedition left the North Dakota area to travel west. She took her baby along, often carrying him on her back. Sacagawea was the only woman to travel with the thirty-three person expedition. Her knowledge of two Native American languages helped the travelers in their encounters with different tribes on their journey. She guided them along some trails she remembered from her childhood, helped find food, and even saved several important items when a canoe capsized.

Lawrence Welk (1903–1992) Lawrence Welk, who was born in a sod house in Strasburg, was the bandleader on his own television show, *The Lawrence Welk Show*. The popular show was televised nationally between 1955 and 1982. The light dance music played by his orchestra became known as champagne music. From 1960 to 1965, his band had twelve records on *Billboard* magazine's weekly Top 100 chart.

Timeline

10,000 BCE	The first humans arrive to hunt woolly mammoth and bison.
1400	Native Americans settle along the Missouri, Knife, and Heart rivers in earth lodges.
1738	French explorer Pierre Gaultier de Varennes, Sieur de La Vérendrye trades with the Mandan.
1804	Lewis and Clark winter at the Mandan camp and meet Sacagawea.
1828	The American Fur Company opens Fort Union.
1861	President James Buchanan establishes the Dakota Territory.
1889	North Dakota becomes the thirty-ninth state.
1901	Theodore Roosevelt becomes president of the United States.
1915	The Non-Partisan League forms.
1918	An influenza epidemic kills 2,700 people statewide.
1929	A severe drought known as the Dust Bowl begins and lasts eight years.
1951	Oil is discovered in western North Dakota.
1956	The Democratic party merges with the Non-Partisan League.
1975	A blizzard kills twelve people statewide and hundreds of cattle.
1988	A severe drought destroys wheat and other crops.
1997	The Red River floods, heavily damaging the Grand Forks area.
2006	Fargo is recognized by the American Lung Association as having some of the cleanest air for any U.S. city of its size.
2007	In January, John Hoeven becomes the nation's longest-serving governor.
2009	Heavy rain and giant ice jams in April cause record flooding along the Red River near Fargo, and at least two die in the flood.
2010	In a time of the highest national unemployment since the Great Depression, where one in ten people are unemployed, North Dakota's unemployment is only 4 percent.

State motto:	"Liberty and Union, Now and Forever, One and Inseparable"
State capital:	Bismarck
State flag:	On a blue field, a bald eagle holds a red ribbon in its beak that reads *E PLURIBUS UNUM* ("Out of many, One"), the motto of the United States. In its talons, the eagle holds seven arrows (defense of liberty) and an olive branch with three red berries (peace). A red, white, and blue shield is on the eagle's body. Above the eagle are thirteen stars (the thirteen colonies) and a yellow fan. Beneath the eagle, on a red scroll, are the words "NORTH DAKOTA." The flag was adopted in 1911.
State tree:	American elm
State bird:	Western meadowlark
State flower:	Wild prairie rose
State fruit:	Chokecherry
Statehood date and number:	November 2, 1889; the thirty-ninth state
State nicknames:	The Peace Garden State, the Flickertail State, the Roughrider State
Total area and U.S. rank:	70,704 square miles (183,122 sq km); nineteenth-largest state

State flag

State seal

Population:	642,200
Highest elevation:	White Butte, 3,506 feet (1,069 m) above sea level
Lowest elevation:	Along the Red River, 750 feet (229 m) above sea level
Major rivers:	Missouri River, Red River, James River, Knife River, Little Missouri River, Sheyenne River, Pembina River, Souris River, Yellowstone River, Heart River, Cannonball River, Cedar Creek
Major lakes:	Lake Sakakawea, Lake Oahe, Lake Tschida, Devils Lake, Alkaline Lake, Horsehead Lake
Highest recorded temperature:	121°F (49°C), July 6, 1936, at Steele
Lowest recorded temperature:	-60°F (-51°C), February 15, 1936, at Parshall
Origin of state name:	*Dakota* is the Sioux word for "friend"
Chief agricultural products:	Wheat, cattle, barley, sugar beets, soybeans
Major industries:	Food processing, machinery, mining, tourism

Western meadowlark

Wild prairie rose

GLOSSARY

advocate A champion or supporter.

agrarian Describing a way of life that involves growing and tending to food.

appeal A legal proceeding by which a case is brought before a higher court to review a decision of a lower court.

basin Usually a large depression on the surface of the land with gradually sloping sides.

bicameral Describing a lawmaking body made up of two legislative houses.

bonanza farm A huge farm, usually for growing wheat, formed to take advantage of very cheap land and efficient plowing and harvesting technologies.

butte A hill, often with vertical sides and a nearly flat top.

diversification A method of minimizing financial risk by selling or investing in more than one type of economic good or service.

dust bowl An area in the United States that suffered from severe dust storms from 1930 to 1936.

electoral college A body of elected representatives that formally elect the president and vice president.

fallow The condition of leaving soil unplanted to allow for the replenishment of nutrients and the breakdown of toxins.

geologist A scientist who studies rocks, including how and when they were formed, the minerals they contain, and how they have changed over time.

gross domestic product (GDP) The value of all goods and services performed within a state or nation for one year.

habitat The kind of environment in which a species or organism lives.

Homestead Act of 1862 A law that granted 160 acres (65 ha) of unoccupied land to anyone who lived on the land for five years.

immigrant A person that moves, usually from one country to a new one, to take up permanent residence.

kettle lake A depression created by partially buried ice blocks as they melted and that filled with water to become a kettle lake.

monopoly The possession or control of the supply or trade in a product or service.

municipality A clearly defined territory within a state that has its own governing body, often a mayor and council.

nomadic A community of people that moves from place to place, often to follow favorable hunting or living conditions, rather than settling permanently in one location.

Non-Partisan League (NPL) A political party formed in North Dakota by socialist leader A. C. Townley that advocated state ownership of banks, mills, and grain elevators.

Northwest Passage A water route connecting the Atlantic and Pacific oceans that runs north of the continent.

predatory Intended to injure or exploit people for personal gain or profit, as in predatory lending or pricing.

price fixing The maintaining of prices to a certain amount by agreement between competing sellers.

reservation Land that has been set aside by the U.S. government and is governed by various Native American tribes.

segregation The enforced separation of different racial groups in a country, community, or establishment.

silt An extremely fine grain of soil often found at the bottom of bodies of water.

sustainable agriculture Farming practices that combine profitability with the conservation of natural resources.

translator Somebody who interprets or translates from one language to another.

watershed The drainage basin of a stream or river.

woolly mammoth A heavy-coated mammoth, a type of extinct elephant that lived in colder areas of the northern hemisphere.

North Dakota Council on the Arts

1600 East Century Avenue, Suite 6

Bismarck, ND 58503-0649

(701) 328-7590

Web site: http://www.nd.gov/arts

The North Dakota Council on the Arts promotes and funds artistic development within the state using state and federal funds. The organization also works to increase access to the arts in schools.

North Dakota Game and Fish Department

100 North Bismarck Expressway

Bismarck, ND 58501-5095

(701) 328-6305

Web site: http://gf.nd.gov

The North Dakota Game and Fish Department helps protect and preserve the fish and wildlife of the state through careful control of licenses and regulations.

North Dakota Nature and Rural Tourism Association

2767 129th Avenue, SW

Belfield, ND 58622-9330

(701) 575-4767

Web site: http://www.ndnature.org

The North Dakota Nature and Rural Tourism Association promotes and preserves rural North Dakota's landscape and diverse cultures.

North Dakota Official Portal for North Dakota State Government

600 East Boulevard Avenue, Department 130

Bismarck, ND 58505-0130

(701) 328-2471

Web site: http://www.nd.gov/category.htm?id=147

This official portal contains links to basic state information on agriculture and economy, history and government, population, and state symbols.

State Historical Society of North Dakota

612 East Boulevard Avenue

Bismarck, ND 58505

(701) 328-2666

Web site: http://history.nd.gov

The State Historical Society of North Dakota collects and preserves the artifacts of North Dakota's history. The society also researches that history and educates people about the history of the state.

Theodore Roosevelt National Park

315 Second Avenue

Medora, ND 58645

(701) 842-2333

Web site: http://www.nps.gov/thro/index.htm

The Theodore Roosevelt National Park maintains Roosevelt's two cattle ranches in the Badlands of North Dakota. The park also works to educate the public on how Roosevelt's time in North Dakota influenced his philosophy and his decisions as U.S. president.

Trail Tribes Regional Learning Project

University of Montana Continuing Education Building

Missoula, MT 59812

Web site: http://www.trailtribes.org/index.html

The Trail Tribes project examines the history of Native American peoples along the route of the Lewis and Clark expedition to the Pacific Ocean.

Web Sites

Due to the changing nature of Internet links, Rosen Publishing has developed an online list of Web sites related to the subject of this book. This site is updated regularly. Please use this link to access the list:

http://www.rosenlinks.com/uspp/ndpp

Burt, Christopher C., and Mark Shroud. *Extreme Weather: A Guide and Record Book*. New York, NY: W. W. Norton & Company, 2007.

Handy-Marchello, Barbara. *Women of the Northern Plains: Gender and Settlement on the Homestead Frontier, 1870–1930*. St. Paul, MN: Minnesota Historical Society Press, 2005.

Harrison, Jim. *The English Major*. New York, NY: Grove Press, 2008.

Herman, Gwyn, and Laverne Johnson. *Frontier Era of North Dakota*. Fargo, ND: North Dakota Center for Distance Education, 2007.

Lazenby, Ronald. *Mindgames: Phil Jackson's Long Strange Journey*. Lincoln, NE: Bison Books, 2007.

Lewis, Meriwether, William Clark, and William Bergon. *The Journals of Lewis and Clark*. New York, NY: Penguin Books, 2003.

Omdahl, Lloyd. *Governing North Dakota*. Grand Forks, ND: University of North Dakota, Bureau of Governmental Affairs, 2005.

Paulsen, Gary. *The Beet Fields: Memories of a Sixteenth Summer*. New York, NY: Laurel Leaf, 2002.

Sanders, Doug. *North Dakota*. Tarrytown, NY: Benchmark Books, 2004.

Silverman, Robin L. *North Dakota* (From Sea to Shining Sea). New York, NY: Scholastic Library Publishing, 2009.

BIBLIOGRAPHY

Bank of North Dakota. "About Lending Services." Retrieved November 3, 2009 (http://www.banknd.nd.gov/bndhome.jsp).

Burns, Ken. "Lewis & Clark: A Journey of the Corps of Discovery." Retrieved October 10, 2009 (http://www.pbs.org/lewisandclark).

Fifer, Barbara. *Everyday Geography of the United States*. New York, NY: Black Dog & Leventhal Publishers, 2003.

Harkinson, Josh. "How the Nation's Only State-Owned Bank Became the Envy of Wall Street." *Mother Jones*, March 2009. Retrieved October 12, 2009 (http://www.motherjones.com/mojo/2009/03/how-nation%E2%80%99s-only-state-owned-bank-became-envy-wall-street).

Hoganson, J. W., and E. C. Murphy. *Geology of the Lewis and Clark Trail in North Dakota*. Missoula, MT: Mountain Press Publishing Company, 2003.

Kitchen, Martin. *A History of Modern Germany, 1800–2000*. New York, NY: Wiley-Blackwell, 2006.

North Dakota. "North Dakota Notes." Retrieved September 11, 2009 (https://www.dmr.nd.gov/ndgs/ndnotes/ndnotes.asp).

Northern Prairie Wildlife Research Center. "Climate of North Dakota." Retrieved October 4, 2009 (http://www.npwrc.usgs.gov/resource/habitat/climate/intro.htm).

Northern Prairie Wildlife Research Center. "North Dakota Furtakers Educational Manual: The History of the Fur Trade in North Dakota." Retrieved September 12, 2009 (http://www.npwrc.usgs.gov/resource/mammals/furtake/history.htm).

Turtle Mountain Band of Chippewa Council. "Area Profile." Retrieved November 18, 2009 (http://www.tmbci.net/index.html).

U.S. Census Bureau. "State and County Quick Facts: North Dakota." Retrieved November 2, 2009 (http://quickfacts.census.gov/qfd/states/38000.html).

Yenne, Bill. *Sitting Bull*. Yardley, PA: Westholme Publishing, 2008.

INDEX

A

Agassiz, Lake, 8
agriculture/farming, 5, 7, 9, 10, 11, 16–17, 22, 25–26, 28
Anderson, Lynn, 30

B

Bank of North Dakota, 22
Bismarck, 9–10, 19, 21, 27
bonanza farms, 25, 28

C

Carlsen, Anne, 30
Christopher, Warren, 33
Crazy Horse, 5, 14

D

Dakota Territory, 5, 12, 15, 28
Davies, Ronald, 32
Devils Lake, 10
Drift Prairie, 6, 9–10

E

Eielson, Carl "Ben," 32
Enabling Act, 16
European settlement, 12, 13
executive branch of government, 19–21

F

family farms, 25, 28
Fargo, 10, 17–18, 24, 27, 37
Farmers Alliance, 17

G

governor, role of, 19–20, 22
Grand Forks, 10, 27, 34, 36

H

Homestead Act, 15–16, 28

I

immigrants, 15–16, 17

J

Jackson, Phil, 5, 34
judicial branch of government, 23–24

L

L'Amour, Louis, 34
legislative assembly, 21–23
Lewis and Clark expedition, 13, 37
lieutenant governor, role of, 20, 23
local government, 24
Lutz, Kellan, 34

M

manufacturing, 26–27, 29
Microsoft, 18
Miller, John, 16
mining, 27–29
Missouri Plateau, 6–9
Missouri River, 6, 12, 14, 15

N

Native Americans, 5, 12, 13, 14, 33, 37
Non-Partisan League, 5, 17, 22
North Dakota State University, 18

P

Purpur, Clifford "Fido," 34–36

R

Red River, 6, 10, 11, 17
Red River Valley, 5, 6, 8, 10–11
Roosevelt, Theodore, 5, 33
Rosenquist, James, 36–37

S

Sacagawea, 13, 37
Sakakawea, Lake, 6, 9
service sector, 29
Sitting Bull, 5, 14, 33
statehood, 16

W

Welk, Lawrence, 37

About the Author

Mark J. Lewis is an education content developer and children's literature writer with five years of teaching experience in high school alternative education programs. He has studied American history, specializing in the Westward Expansion and the Civil War era.

Photo Credits

Cover (top left) © www.istockphoto.com/Cheryl A. Meyer; cover (top right) Medioimages/Photodisc/Getty Images; cover (bottom) Jeff Foott/Discovery Channel Images/Getty Images; pp. 3, 6, 12, 19, 25, 30, 38 Annie Griffiths Belt/National Geographic/Getty Images; p. 4 (top) © GeoAtlas; p. 7 Dirk Anschutz/Stone/Getty Images; pp. 9, 40 (right) Shutterstock.com; p. 11 Andrew Sacks/Time & Life Pictures/Getty Images; p. 13 Private Collection/The Bridgeman Art Library/Getty Images; pp. 15, 26 Fred Hultstrand History in Pictures Collection, NDIRS-NDSU, Fargo; p. 16 Buyenlarge/Hulton Archive/Getty Images; p. 18 Daniel Barry/Getty Images; p. 20 Newscom; pp. 21, 32, 35 © AP Images; p. 27 AFP/Getty Images; p. 28 Geoffrey Clifford/Photographer's Choice/Getty Images; p. 31 Rick Diamond/Getty Images; p. 36 Bloomberg via Getty Images; p. 39 (left) Courtesy of Robesus, Inc.; p. 40 (left) © www.istockphoto.com/Stephen Muskie

Designer: Les Kanturek; Editor: Kathy Kuhtz Campbell
Photo Researcher: Peter Tomlinson